forgiveness

channeled work by The Teachers

forgiveness

the attraction series

book 2

CAROL COLLINS
channel for The Teachers

SP
SYNERGISTIC PUBLISHING

Synergistic Publishing
Alexandria, Virginia

Forgiveness. Book 2 of The Attraction Series.
2023 by Carol Collins

Published by Synergistic Publishing
synergistic-publishing.com

Cover Design: Carol Collins

Channeling sessions for this book were recorded in 3 sessions for a total duration of 3 hours. All content was recorded by video and uploaded to a transcription service. Only grammatical edits were made.

The intent of the author is to provide general information to individuals who are taking positive steps towards emotional and spiritual well-being. Synergistic Publishing is proud to offer this channeled book.

The Teachers of Jeshua (Spirit)
Forgiveness / [channeled by] Carol Collins.
"Wisdom from Beyond."

ISBN: 979-8-9886421-2-1 (paperback)
ISBN: 979-8-9886421-3-8 (ebook)
First Edition: January 2024

MIND BODY SPIRIT / Psychology

books by The Teachers

with recommended reading order
Ocularity of the Mind (2022)
Mind Body Connection (2022)
Manifestation of the True Self (2022)

The Attraction Series (2023)

The Unfoldment Logbook (2023)

The Essential Material
The Four Pillars of Learning

PILLAR 1: The Foundational Material – the starting point for understanding who your Guide is and why we are having a life. All Pillar One material aligns to and heals the Sacrum Chakra.

PILLAR 2: Idea Reconstruction - otherwise known as law of attraction, deliberate creation, and using the power of thought energy to manifest your life, on purpose. All Pillar Two material aligns to and heals the Throat Chakra.

PILLAR 3: Self-Healing – moving Source Frequency within "The Grid" as a means of clearing unconscious beliefs that stop and/or delay your ability to connect with your Guide team and manifest a life of abundance. All Pillar Three material aligns to and heals the Root Chakra.

PILLAR 4: Intuitive Advancement – verbal and vibrational instruction to open your inter-mind to ocular (mind's eye) to increase your ability to receive, clarity in that receiving, and accuracy on what your Guide is conveying to you. All Pillar Four material aligns to and heals the Crown Chakra.

a pillar 2 book

dedication

For my daughters,
Elizabeth, Emma, and Amanda

To be in alignment is what you were born to be, to learn, to think about. You are doing it. You are living it. You are making a difference. I love that!

Contents

introduction

My dear readers,

How many ways are there to say I love you? Endless, unless you limit yourself to those three words. I want you to know that when I say I love you, I mean I care about you — fully. The world says, I love you as they are crying, as they are pleading, as they are grieving. You cannot love and plead at the same time.

What you are truly saying is, I am terrified to not have you in my life, I do not know my own identity strong enough to be safe without you by my side. I want you to feel that way about no human being.

I want no human being to have you wound so tightly that you fear moving forward without them.

I want you to know that love is a feeling of passion, desire, gentle view, and joy all wrapped together. What I teach is what love is. Perfect balance, beautiful interaction. The world teaches dis- similar because the world has an emotional range that is different than mine.

I want you to adore people, to adore life, to adore your surroundings and want for nothing save more of what you have. I want you to feel depth of that every moment of every day. This small book offers exercises. I encourage you to do them as you are reading the book. You will get the most out of it if you do. You will gain understanding even if you do not, but you will alter the mini you on the inside that decides whether you will be someone who says I love you while pleading or I adore this moment while you are smiling. It, in other words, needs adjustment.

The exercises are short but meaningful. I chose the word forgiveness because it is what the subconscious mind needs to be able to hear us clean, clear, and accurate. When you forgive yourself for what the world subjects you to you are, in essence, choosing love, true love — just love.

The inner mind is the subconscious. It holds on to everything. It wants forgiveness for everything that is less than what you truly are, a Love Being. You are meant to give love, see love, feel love, breathe love, experience love. It knows it. It does not know what to do with harsh emotions, so it files them away and they turn into what the world now calls stress.

Stress manifests as a negative attribute, always. There are many ways to undo internalized stress. I'll give you a few playful ways — do recognize that playfulness is the operative word.

Be at ease. Enjoy the stories. Highlight, underline, write in the margins because when you do, you are also telling that interior you that you like forgiveness for yourself from what the world has done through the word love because it has taught you poorly.

We teach you and we give you our love, always.

~ One among The Teachers

forgiveness

chapter one

We have a playful way when speaking through this woman, Carol. It's the way her own "gifts" developed. She's a playful one, but it's also how we want you all to be when you have conversations with us.

What you call clairvoyance is what we call ocularity. We like that term best and we want you to have conversations with us. We don't want you to pray to us. We don't want you to have idols. We don't want you to have statues. We don't want you to have memories of history books. We want you to not worry about what people say about you. We want you to not say things about other people that cause the m to worry. But you will, without a doubt because you are a human being.

We don't expect you to be perfect. There is no expectation from your Guide nor us. But we do have a preference, and we prefer that you are full of joy. We prefer that you appreciate life. We prefer that you look around your homes and your families and your workplaces and find things to feel good about.

Who are we? We are The Teachers of Jeshua, a collective of beings that have lived many lives and now teach you. We speak from a perspective that you are not aware of — not grandeur, not ghostly, not spirited, although we can be very funny if you allow us to be.

This woman, Carol, it's a Tuesday evening and she's had a delightful day. She's sitting here on her rosebud furniture. It's not full of rosebuds but it is an ash rose color, very soft, nice extra wide chair.

She's curled up with her pink rose colored blanket on top of her and she's hearing her cat scratch on the scratch pad that she purchased at Petco.

She's in the middle of painting this new home of hers a color that feels better than the one it came with. There's a flagpole right outside, almost eye level because we're on the second floor of a three-story town home. She is getting ready to sell this townhome, although she's only lived in it nearly three months. Why is she selling it? Because of a con- versation she had with us about how to accumulate wealth.

She follows where we lead her. We do not lead you astray, none of you. But some of you don't hear us clearly. Some of you don't know this, but receivers you all are. You're born with it. It is part of the experience as a human being, to have the ability for conversations with us.

It's not a failsafe button. It is a switch that is merely on all the time. This switch, it never fully turns off. It's one of those light switches that just doesn't work properly meaning you can turn it on, but you can never turn it off. The darndest thing about it, no matter what you do, you just can't turn it off.

There's always a healing frequency flowing to you and through you in other words every moment of every day throughout your entire life, whether you hear us verbally in the mind, see picture books in the mind, or feel sensations or other ways of communicating with us.

Carol is a channeled medium. We describe her that way. She describes herself as having this really cool gift of being able to talk to her nonphysical teachers, and that she loves it so much.

Not fifteen-minutes ago, we were having a conversation with her where we were giving her partial sentences and she was completing the prompt. It's a way of playful learning, and it's the best way to improve your ability to hear us.

When you learn mediumship or channeling in a classroom that is full of exercises, you experience — try this exercise and see what you get, practice with a partner and see what you get, tell us what you got...

The mind learns this: that you want to have a conversation with your Guide, but it also wants to please you and when you practice, and the mind has not yet been prepared for the length of the conversation that you are wanting to have, the mind must simulate the conversation and substitute itself for us.

You wonder, some of you, when you sit and receive personal guidance or offer your gift to others why that the information does not manifest or is not validated.

Sometimes the mind makes a mess of receiving and translating. It always introduces its own concept of reality into the conversation. Sometimes so much so that the intended conversation is lost.

Every once in a while, a human being becomes quieted in the mind to such a degree that the inner mind rests fully when we are passing conversation to it. So fully that the mind simply registers that a conversation is taking place and has little need to introduce its own information into the stream of received thought.

It is as if it sits back and reads the news-paper while the conversation is occurring. It knows the conversation is happening, but it does not take possession of it as something that it needs to control, that it needs to participate in. Although at times this inner mind does have an interest in what is being shared. If so, the mind listens but does not interject into it. That is a well-tended for mind.

We teach the mind, you tend to it by your thoughts, by your actions, by your playtime activities, what you engage in, whether you shout at your neighbor or invite them over for dinner, whether you get down on yourself for waking up late or whether you delight in having slept in — no matter if it's the first time or the tenth in a row.

A quieted mind is nicer to others and to yourself. Simply this, quieted is you in the moment, the here and now, how you are behaving and how you are thinking. It's the example that you set in that exact moment. The example that you set can change from moment to moment, and it often does.

A mind that does not interject into the conversation that we are having through a human being is a mind that is both soft and supple. Soft means that it loves us. The interior mind knows who we are, and it loves us so much that it desires our company. It knows us from all other vibrational thought forms. It identifies us as real and it loves us and it knows that we are speaking to it, specifically.

A supple mind is one that is quiet, meaning outwardly gentle. When you have soft and supple together, you have the beautiful combination of what is necessary for us to speak through you in the way of a full and open channel.

How do you get there? Desire for a kinder world, for a gentler nation, to look about and see things in a different way, in a way that is not harsh or critical or full of judgment. You care about how to do something, but you're less concerned about the outcome and more interested in how you got there. Curiosity abounds everywhere, you're playful, you're happy, although not necessarily angelic.

We want you to have interests and passions, but the things that you are wanting to compromise your life no longer consist of guns, vulgar comedies, incestuous things, or any violence. Petty squabbles no longer interest you. Human rights might, but your involvement is only to the point of supportive, not inciting a riot. You care about the planet and about those that inhabit it, all things. You might take care of your home differently than you once did. You see the flora and fauna as living things and you speak to it as a way of nurturing the spirit within. You believe not only in the cosmos, but in the powerfulness of Source, and you know, without a shadow of a doubt that there is life after life.

When we talk about forgiveness some- times there is a misunderstanding because we also say there is no sin and we love everything about you. How can we give these messages through so many of joy, of hope, of seeing the way we see the world and yet give you our knowing that many of you do not take care of yourselves, nor the planet, that you seek love but you do not invest yourself in being able to communicate in a way that brings about lengthy relationships?

If there is no sin, and there is not, then why is there a need for forgiveness? Because there is a need to know that you are loved.

When you know that you are loved then you no longer hold on to shame.

We want you to look in the mirror. If you're playful, you will find a mirror at this moment. Look right in the mirror and say, "Who am I? Who am I? Who am I?" until a thought forms in your mind about who you are. What does that inner mind say when you focus your eyes upon yourself and ask that very basic question, "Who am I?"

In a very real way, you are asking your interior mind to tell you what you think about yourself. A variety of words may come as a result of this exercise. We want you to write them down and we want you to examine not your consciousness, and also not your behavior, but your emotional response to the words. Do you feel sad?

Do you feel sensational? Sensitivity training is one way to improve the thought pattern of the interior mind.

Sensitivity training is learning how to name the emotion that you are feeling segment by segment by segment of your day. Expand your vocabulary.

Emotional words and their definition play a part in how you look about the world. Words have a definition; they also have a connotation. The connotation changes from person to person, but the definition does not.

You are, most of you, aware of this. Both definition and connotation have meaning to the interior mind, as well as tone. Flippant, sarcastic, serious, playful — the mind registers all of them differently, even if the same word is used consecutively.

When you say you are angry, are you truly disappointed, disgusted, annoyed, or unusually overwhelmed? When you expand your vocabulary, you offer the interior mind an alternative to the word that you may have otherwise chosen quickly. In that way the interior mind learns verbally as well as vibrationally.

Vocabulary has with it attributes that you can describe. The way you say a certain word, whatever the word is, has artificial connotation. That artificial connotation is what the mind takes in, labels it with your name, and says, "This is me. I am _____." It has a filing cabinet labeled "Who I Am." When you do the mirror exercise the mind reaches into that filing cabinet and it selects words based on the kinds of emotional things you have been paying attention to – be it playful, happy, disappointed, or unauthorized.

All right let's stop there. If you're playing this game and you have a word like unauthorized show up in your mind's eye, substitute guilt, inferior, scared of consequences, inadequate, derelict, truant, late, tardy, or anti-disestablishment.

The word that arrives first is a folder in this cabinet and in the folder are all the synonyms.

All of those synonyms are how the mind describes you based on the kinds of things that you do or think or say or participate in or watch or listen to. Ingest, in other words.

If you have a dictionary handy look up the word that came to your mind and look at the list of synonyms. Those are the words that you believe about yourself.

Who am I? One word equals many. This one-to-many relationship equals how you think about yourself.

The inner psyche of the mind is described, and it is the one who captures, holds, retains, and memorizes all of the wayward thoughts that you have ever had. Not only the wayward, but also the positive. You may have, upon completing this exercise, had something like happy-go-lucky arise from the depths of your knowing that describe you. The exercise is the same, there is a folder with these positive attributes and all of their synonyms in this filing cabinet labeled Who I Am. There are drawers and drawers full of word connotation, relational descriptors of you, as authored by your interior mind.

We want you, the awake, aware, exoconscious part of you to relearn vocabulary so that you can reteach the interior mind who you are wanting to be — superfluous, anticlimactic, wrongdoer, pleaser, schizophrenic, heart attack recipient, varicose vein potential, geez I just don't know, why I can't remember.

The words that you use to describe yourself are taken in and filed according to the vibrational tone within them. The mind knows, "I hate you" (smile face) from "I hate you" (angry face). The words do not necessarily matter, but oftentimes they do.

If you have a thesaurus, you will find even more descriptors, both synonyms and antonyms. If you have a word slowly arise into your mind that you agree with, then look at all the synonyms and say, "This is me, this is me, this is me!" and become more excited with each repetition. Then look up the synonyms to those words and increase your knowing of who your mind thinks you are based on what life experience has taught it.

Now, conversely, if a word floats in and it does not please you then you have work to do. Do not, however, look up all the synonyms and then the synonyms of those synonyms to find one that fits better because that only reinforces the decision that your mind has made about who you think you are based on the words that you have used about yourself and the activities that you have engaged in.

Instead, look at the antonyms. Disregard the word that did not please you and find the opposite, many opposites and delight in knowing that there are opposites.

You are not angry; it is not who you are. You are not depressed; it is not who you are. You are not cataclysmic; it is not who you are. Petty, it is not who you are. Hamster in a cage, it is not who you are. Although it might be the likeness of who you have been at some moment in time. A moment does not describe anything fully.

You are love, in other words.

Know this clearly, there is no angry human being. There are many human beings who have suffered from infliction to the point where they have an outburst which is then categorized and labeled by others as angry. If someone is picked on often enough in front of others to the point where they lash back, opinions may be formed based on observation of tiny segments of that person's life, or the accumulation of these segments.

Label no one as an emotion unless it is powerfully positive. Label yourself not in the same way.

How often should one do this type of exercise? Once. This is a one-time exercise. If you follow through on your research of antonyms or synonyms, depending on the case, no further investigation of the mind is needed because in that moment, you will have retaught it and reinforced it with who you are or who you are wanting to be. Both equal who you are in either event.

You recreate yourselves every time you speak. Let the last word that you have about yourself be positive.

chapter two

If you are wanting to know what we think about your life, ask us. We will tell you plainly where you are, what you are currently manifesting, where to emphasize your current thinking, your current beingness, and where a U-turn might be necessary.

We do not mix words. We love you very much but we do not love everything that you do. We do not love hate and discontent. We do not love gnashing of teeth. We do not love how you behave sometimes, but we love you, always.

That is how we want you to view your own life. "I like what I said very much, I think I'm going to say that again and again, it felt magnanimous."

We want you to increase your vocabulary so that you can describe yourself in different ways. We want you to be happy about who you are. We want you to have a fun time with this thing called life. We want you to have a plethora of descriptors that please you. You do not, to quote a phrase you use, need to be a rocket scientist in all things but we do want you to have a swift and easy time moving about emotionally. Diversity in emotional descriptions of yourself creates that.

The more words that you know, the less the interior mind snatches onto a single descriptor and says, "This is me!" This is especially useful for all of those negative thought patterns. The quantity, the frequency, and the tone all matter.

If on occasion you have mood swings and when you do you really get down on yourself and you dive into emotional dispositions that are conveyed verbally to others or to yourself, then you are in Group A, occasionally disagreeable.

If you are someone that is generally disagreeable, not hot-tempered but also not cool-tempered, the tone you use is generally similar from one day to the next and is also consistently negative, you are Group B.

Which one of these — Group A or Group A?

Stop here for a moment. Examine where your mind just went. We did not make a mistake, but the mind jumped forward in thought. Where did it go? Write that down as exercise number two. Did you finish the sentence? Did you register that Group A was spoken twice? If so did you want to contradict it? Did you pause and get curious about why that phrase was spoken twice? Did you immediately criticize and think we made a mistake or that the publisher did? Were you playful and cheery or were you critical? In either event, now go to the second part of the first exercise and do the synonym/antonym work again. Do this exercise fully one time.

If you did not do the mirror game and simply read the words, we want you to pause here and keep your place until you have a moment to do both exercise one and two back-to-back. This will be telling to you about where you are in your state of beingness. Are you positive-positive? Are you positive-negative? Are you negative-positive? Are you negative-negative?

If positive-positive, do more of it. Expand your vocabulary so that you can play even further with describing who you are. This will help you manifest more and different.

Are you positive-negative? If so, the interior mind believes that you are positive, but your current state of mind is negative. In that case, be at ease but clean it up a bit on this minute scale.

If you were negative-positive there is some work to be done in how you think about yourself because the interior mind is showing you what is predominant within you.

How do you clean that up? Stop watching television, put video games down, stop playing the lottery, a sarcastic tone with others, try your best not to. Read, but nothing that invokes anger, such as: the Bible, War and Peace, epic novel about battles, romance novels that describe infidelity and the human frailty. Instead, occupy your time with doodling, painting, walking, getting a massage, painting your nails, building something from scratch whether it be a puzzle or a deck matters not. Play games, talk to your children, eat well to include leafy greens. Make your plates colorful and alive with the variety, whether it be spices, sauces, or the like. If you care not for leafy greens, try a cucumber slice. Allow the palate to enhance itself. Explore textures, flavors, heat. Walk outdoors. Remove politics altogether because external life has a way of influencing you.

You may think that happy-go-lucky ought to have been the word or the phrase that floated up during the mirror game — and perhaps you are that. But the influences that are generally around you are starkly or vastly different from that view that you have of yourself. The interior mind is still correct. That what you think about, you become.

Whether you realize it or not, those transitory conversations, those background noises called television and music, are influencers. If your ears hear it, then the mind assumes you want it, that you are it, and that you want to become it. And so it brings it to you.

If the second exercise brought about positive, it means that on the surface, that is you. Do more of it. When you reduce — or eliminate, which is preferred all of those other influences, you will become positive-positive after a while.

If you are in the fourth group, negative-negative, meditation is required to reverse the thought pattern of the interior mind. Meditation may include a variety of things. Quiet meditation is but one, coloring is another. Washing the floor, whether it's with a mop or with a scrub brush on your hands and knees, is another. Laying on a blanket in a park setting feeling the breeze and the sunshine on your face, is yet another. Eating flavorful foods slowly and appreciating the taste or the concept of how the flavors were put together, can be another. Reducing the number of chores that you have given for yourself for any single day, is another.

Slow down, destress, unwind. If you enjoy bubble baths, do them often. If you enjoy scented candles, light them and allow the aroma or the beauty of it to enhance how you feel about the room that you are in. Become someone that takes time out of each day to journal about something that sets your soul on fire with passion, joy, and love.

You are creating your reality in every- thing you say and everything you do. You are teaching the mind, the interior mind, who you are wanting to be, and then it brings it to you.

Some of you know this, most do not, or are unsure how the interior mind brings life experiences to you. What you think about you get more of. Be at ease and be at peace, but also know those words are true. Don't go over- board and try to reverse everything all at once. You will create dysfunction in the mind and then you will have stress in your life.

Change one or two things until they feel comfortable and then add another. Then another and then another. Slowly over time, you will have reversed enough that the interior mind will become quieted. And then, you just might be able to hear us or those like us that are guiding you, ocularly.

chapter three

A quieted mind can sometimes hear us. A soft mind can hear us in the moment. A supple mind creates clarity. When you have any combination of these then you may receive guidance occasionally for yourself.

Know this to be true, human beings are not quieted. You have quiet moments, but you are not quieted. Quieted is a state of being. We want you all to be quieted, but yet have a ruckus or two on occasion. Be flamboyant, be bold and brave and beautiful while also meek and mild tempered in your behavior, insulated from criticism.

Judge not, but if you are, forgive yourself for noticing because if you are in alignment with us and someone has unplayful, critical comments towards you, you will not notice such things in the future.

You create your reality. If someone is unkind towards you, and you are in alignment with us, you will not know of it or it will be apparent that they are unkind. But you will also not feel the pain of the intendedness within the comment. When you are happy you are in alignment with Source, the Universe, with Us, and your Guide.

You have many names for us, who we are and what we are. We have but one, Consciousness. Be not afraid to ask for our help. We do hear you, and we always answer.

Ask it of us, and we will answer. Ask it in general, and your Guide answers, always. But ask for help, that is what we do after all.

Be playful, have a good time in life. Argue not for longer than is necessary and let it not be felt or seen or ingested as an argument — healthy debate are better words. That is what vocabulary can do for you.

When you look back on a healthy debate, your mind views it differently, even if you called it an argument five minutes or five years before. Change your history by changing your vocabulary. Describe things in a different way and the mind relearns what it learned about the same moment in time. Words are powerful, and so are you.

Be at peace with who you are and know that there's always an opportunity for growth. Grow in the direction of wanted. If growth. Grow in the direction of wanted. If that means a U-turn, make it, and make it wide. When you do, you will not tax the mind and cause it to bring about stressful circumstances to you.

Doing too much, too quickly puts pressure on the interior mind. It cannot handle too much. It fights back and gives you circumstances that cause you to need a time out. That could be illness, it could be oversleeping, it could be lethargy.

Picture teaching a teenager how to drive. If you give them the motor vehicle department's book of knowledge and give them an hour to learn it and take them for their paper test and then the road test right after it, and they've never had an opportunity to flip through the book before that moment, they will fail. They will be frightened. They will learn some things, but they won't know if the things that they learned will be on the test. They will feel unconfident. They might have excitement at the challenge, but the likelihood of passing is slim.

Don't pressure yourself to be perfect at this. You will emphasize that which you are wanting to change. When you make a narrow U-turn you are being unkind to yourself. Give yourself time to adjust, and it will not take long before the mind is eager for more. The mind enjoys happy more than anything else. It feels proud when it feels happy, and pride is necessary for creating a life of abundance.

Soothe the mind with pleasant things while you are making this wide U-turn. Compliment yourself on embarking on this journey of changing your ways, changing your thoughts, changing your habits. A bicep that has not received specific exercise and then is exercised to the point of exhaustion, needs a recovery period. Do not induce a required recovery session for the mind. Give it a little at a time, and it will respond quicker.

Whatever you think about, you get. If you think you are being loving to yourself, it, the interior mind, will respond in kind in what manifests as your life. It's amazing how it happens, really.

We delight in teaching you about these things. Are we talking about the law of attraction? Yes. Are we talking about the law of creating? Yes. Are we talking about your life? Yes. As it was meant to be? Yes.

You came here once upon a time as a little baby to have a good time, to learn how to move about in this world without believing that you are less than, or more than, another. To experience life and all this world has to offer with neutrality not. Joy at the having done it, always.

We do have a fondness for human beings. We do have a fondness for the human race. That means all humans, all of them on your social media platforms, all in your neighborhoods, all your communities, all up and coming artists, all of you garage band people still working on who you want to become, all of you pharmaceutical representatives or aspiring doctors, nurses included, teachers of any kind, children who are elbowing their position in line at school, vying for the right seat on the swing set among their peers on the playground, construction workers and their colored hats, women who are trying to step into a sector of the population that they are traditionally not welcome. The list goes on.

We love each and every one of you. We love populated areas. We love quiet walks in the park. We love row- boats and sailboats and yachts alike. We love pastimes like golf and tennis and frisbee throwing, kite flying, and bird watching.

We like the human race. We find physical life fascinating.

We enjoy being among you from the dimension where we are speaking from. We enjoy watching you grow and learn and play. We loved stepping into the human form which we have not done in quite some time. However, there may come a time where we decide to engage in human life in that way again. If and when we do, we will hope to learn the lessons that we are now teaching you.

We love how the human frame is big or little, seemingly delicate but not. All of you are like a coin, two-sided: "I am happy, I am unhappy, I am emotionally weak, I am confident and strong. I am interested in this, I am uninterested in that. I have, yet I have not. I desire, yet I don't know if it's right for me. Where do I go? Who do I speak to? How do I know if I'm on the right path?"

We want you to know that we teach you how to be on the right path. We teach you that words matter, that your emotional countenance matters, your ability to be flexible matters, your ability to look around you and make a decision of what you think is best for you at that moment, on that subject, on that day matters.

We say every moment that you are breathing is a moment that you <u>get</u> to decide. This life is so fun, this world is so fun. Just look around you. There are so many things to look at — there are creepy crawly things, there are flying winged things, there are walk about things, there are tall things, there are growing things, there are sturdy things, there are wobbly things, there are pretty sparkly things, there are buzzing things, there are decaying things.

We want you to look about and love them all because it's fascinating to watch. It's fascinating to watch a creepy crawly bug move with such precision. It's fun to watch a child work a math problem out. You can look at them and know that they are focused on nothing else. We want you to be like that. We want you to focus so intently, so specifically, that that one thing captures your attention and then we want you to move away from it easily.

When you do finish the math problem or finish the yard work, we want you to then move into your next best thing.

We want you to leave the previous best thing behind, except for the knowing that you did it well.

Your parents might say you did it half-hearted. We don't. You did it and you did it with as much fulfillment or gusto that you chose to muster in that moment in time. We don't compare you to a different moment in time, so don't compare yourself.

If your parents do or your spouse does, or your partner or your work friends do, well, that's not us. We are the model. We are the ones that you should look to as an example. We do not judge. We will tell you how to do things even better, but we don't compare you amongst your peers or to your own history.

In this moment, you are amazing. You could be on your knees fearful, but at this moment, you are amazing because you are here in this world, in this life, in this body, and you are doing this thing called incarnation.

You don't think of it that way. We do. We think it's fascinating the way the energies were formed about yourself, around yourself and then pinpointed to a specific location — that's a good way to put it —

and found this specific human being and brought yourself into perfect alignment with what was needed to deposit yourself within that human being and then spring forth life.

You've done it and you are doing it. The human being that is you is waking up and living life, going to sleep day after day. We want you to know that we know who you really are. We know the Source Being that is you. We also know what your life is like and what things you are trying to create.

We teach you that you have within you everything that is needed. That does not mean that you have completed all of your life's education, it means that everything is inside of you. There is a deeper part of you that is connected to your Guide and that Guide is powerful. They know everything that you are needing to know in this lifetime. Not just in this moment in time, but in the entirety of your life, they know what you need to know. They communicate it to you, but you do not hear it.

We also find it fascinating that the world, the human race, has evolved itself in this way — to be wayward. It's not bad, nor is it good. It's just how human beings evolved themselves, and we find it fascinating.

We do have a job to do, and that job is to help you in many ways. When you ask us to step in, to intercede, to help, to assist, to guide, we always do. We know when it is you calling on us. We know when our specific name is being used. We know in that moment what you are asking for. We know that you are vibrational Beings and communicators back to our dimension. You don't know this either, but we hear everything you say.

We want you to hear what we say in return. We do not sit back idly waiting for you to ask us a question, we are involved in your lives. But, when you do ask — then we have a delightful conversation amongst ourselves in order to give you what you are asking for in the way that satisfies you fully.

Most of you — we speak in world population terms — don't sense us. If you are reading this book, you might. Out of the billions of people on this planet, it is a smaller percentage that will find their way to this book initially. Those numbers will increase. They will become noticeable. But still, overall, even those that find their way to this book and read it cover to cover there's still a smaller percentage that have learned to perceive us, to sense us, that can communicate with us.

We are helping the world to undo some of what you have done. You have evolved yourself into a race of people that cannot hear us. We are wanting you to hear us. We do one thing that you cannot — we fix the interior mind. Does that make us your savior? It does. But you are also your own savior because you are the one that has to forgive and heal enough to be able to ask us first.

You have to open yourself. Those of you that ask, if you shut down afterwards, we will continue knocking on the door, but you must open it. When you do, keep it open which means, stay interested, learn more, understand what communicating with us is all about — and understand what the chakratic system is all about. The two go hand-in-hand in healing your minds from unconscious beliefs.

We love the human population. We love people. We love continents. We love where you live. We love that you get to live. We love that you are living. We love that you are choosing. We love that you are moving about this fantastic world and learning and teaching and doing and making things and getting excited about things and falling off your bike because you have a bike. We want you to look at that scraped knee and say to us, "Heal me, use the powerfulness that you have within and heal this scrape. I know you can. This world has many things in it, but there's nothing in this world that you cannot do."

We want you to say it with a belief that is so strong that you erase doubt. Then you'll be one of the ones that looks down on that scrape and says, "Where did it go? I had it a moment ago."

Yes, the body heals. How? We have a part to play in that, a big part. How do the cells regenerate? We have a part in that, a very big part. Who among you believes in the powerfulness of Source? Who among you? Some.

You are human beings and there is doubt within you, but some of you have a small amount of doubt. So small, in fact, that depending on the subject there are things that do not touch you, do not bother you. We want the numbers of you that believe that we can heal all things to increase, and we want the frequency of your asking us to help you to increase.

We want you to have everything that you want to have. We want you to be human beings that move about easily. We want you to have a thought pattern that does not include frustration, that does not include depression, that does not include suicidal thoughts.

There is no behavioral tendency. There's one thought, and then you might have had another. You might have had a third or fourth. You might have had a number of them. That does not equal tendency to us because we do not categorize you in a way that is unhealthy.

We say in that moment, you sure did have an unhealthy thought and then you moved away from it. If you point out another occurrence, we would say, yes, you sure did and then you moved away from it. Then we would say, is there something that we can do for you? We want you to be able to say, "Yes, that seems to be a pattern. I want the pattern to subside. Help the pattern to upright itself." Then we look at the pattern and we look at you and we help you. There is no order of difficulty.

There are so many examples, some seemingly small, some seemingly large. We want you to start with something that you have very little doubt in and ask for our help and then watch it take care of itself. Do not step in. Watch it take care of itself. Begin with something that does not have a lot of meaning to you, because when you look at something, when you watch something and you're waiting for resolution, your focus on it adds tension around it and then delay occurs.

If you choose something that is very meaningful for you, you add attention to it in the same way. We want you to start with small things, "Help me to choose my actions in a way that causes me to feel better about them." Now, that's a nice general asking because you make a lot of decisions each and every day.

Ask us to help you to make decisions that feel good, and then step back and watch how many things do feel good. Notice where your decisions don't weigh on you, the time it takes for you to decide is not lengthy, where there's no heartburn as you are moving into a final decision. You simply look at what you have in front of you, and you say, "I think and therefore, I know." Done.

Attribute nothing to yourself in those situations because in that moment, we are helping you. When you say, "Thank you, Teachers, for helping me" or thank you to your Guide, you train your inner mind that you are wanting our help, that you are wanting to rely on us to help you and not the ego mind.

When you rely on the ego mind, it finds all kinds of solutions. Nare one of them is what we would choose because we choose consistently from love and wisdom. It chooses whatever it finds that suits your mood.

We find what is needed for you and then we bring it to you, it is altogether different.

It learns to step aside and allow us to step in. If sidestepping the inner mind causes you joy, then it happily opens the door whenever you ask for us. Sparks of intuition are the result initially and then, suddenly, things are happening all around you that are satisfying, that feel good, that feel easier, on their way to being easy.

You have no idea why life gets difficult, but you also don't know how to make it easier. You don't have to change anything - your relationship or your job or even your shoes. You simply need to change who you are asking for help, yourself or us.

When you ask yourself, the mind challenges itself to create an answer that will satisfy the components that it thinks that you are wanting. When you ask us, we look at who you are, we speak to the Guide of you, and decide what to implement and then we bring it to you.

All you need to do is sit back, relax and receive this silver platter. Your Guide does exactly what we are describing every moment of every day for you. You get to ask us in addition to them.

So many of you say that it's not that easy, that you pray all the time. We are not talking about praying. Prayer is asking for help but there's no expectation of truly receiving it. We want you to ask yourself, "Do I believe that Source beings, Godly beings, the Divine within me is real? Do I know that Source beings are powerful or do I just believe that there's some kind of life after this earthly life?"

If you don't know how powerful we are, then find out. We know all things. We are infinite intelligence and we are here to help you.

Why does it seem like your prayers don't get answered? Because you don't focus on allowing us to do it. In one moment, you ask something of us and in the next moment, you're off trying to find a solution, making phone calls, and tracking down people, banging on doors, fretting, worrying unnecessarily. Ask, pause after, decide to distract yourself and while you do, we use that shift of focus, that shift of energy to bring a solution to your mind.

Who are The Teachers of Jeshua? We are beings who have mastered life in the physical world and then some. Among us are masters of specific things. There are those of us that have mastered all things and those that have mastered some things.

When a being has mastered a subject, we like to describe it as being at the twelfth level for that subject — among the twelfth level entities. When you have mastered all subjects you are of twelve, whole and complete. Until then, you are still on your way.

We want you to use that as an analogy for your own life. Some things you know, some things you don't, some things you're interested in, some things you're not. Some things you gravitate towards easily and some things you don't.

Instead of, "I like it, I like it not" say in- stead, "I prefer this right now." Leave open the opportunity and the potential to expand the variety of things to have an interest in. That's growth. We want you to be able to grow and live your lives fully and discover new things. If you didn't like it yesterday, you just might like it today.

Worry not about where your life is going. Worry not about how you got where you are. Worry not about who talks about you or did or who might and simply say, "What am I wanting   to do today?" If you made a faux pas with someone yesterday carry it not with you any further. If you do, look at it and set it down and be on your way as many times as is needed. Always ask us to help you set it down and leave it where it belongs, in your so-called past so that you can look forward and behave forward, to allow more things that are of forward to come into your experience, things that you like, things that you're wanting, things that will make you happy.

We want you to run around and have a ruckus and enjoy every minute of it and then kick back and say, "Oh! I can't wait to do that again." Let that be your Monday or Tuesday or Wednesday or Thursday or Friday or Saturday or Sun- day. Each of them. You need not have an expectation of having a dreadful Monday, nor swamped Friday.

These terms that you use, stop. Capture the moment and let the moment capture you. Let that be the way you live your life. Create a moment and let that moment capture your attention and then create another moment and let that one capture your attention.

We want you to say things like, "I love this day, it's my favorite day of the week" and then the next day comes and you say, "I love this day, it is my favorite day of the week" and let it not matter to you if you said the same thing yesterday. No guilt, no guilt, no guilt, no guilt. I love this day, it's my favorite day of the week because you are fully focused on that day and that day only.

Compared it to no others and com- pare it to no one else's day. Let it be your day and in that moment, you are alive fully. We want you to have no half-hearted days, no half-hearted lives, no half-hearted conversations, no half-hearted moments. Be present, be fully present. Enjoy it like no other each and every time. How do you do that? Choose to.

We know so many of you ask us to give you something more tangible to work with. We say, "OK." Then you ask us what it is and we say, "Ask us for help." When you ask us for help, your inner mind allows the answer to come to you that we were giving all along. That's what we do. You ask, we give.

Sit back and receive and then think of something else that you want. Then ask again so we can give again and we get to have a grand old time for your entire life. That's the way life is meant to be. That's the way it is - you just don't see it that way or integrate us into your lives. But you can.

We have full faith in you. We know that you sometimes have faith in yourself. Keep it going. We want you to feel good today and every day. Let that be the thing that you wake up to and that you fall asleep to. "I can't wait for this day" and "I had a

great day." Let that be your start and your finish no matter what the hours in between held within it. In that way you are creating so many things that you are wanting more of.

chapter four

So now we talk about forgiveness. How does forgiveness play into your ability to see things in a way that make you feel better? Simply this, forgive or for- give not, which one feels better?

Ask yourself this, "How do I move away from a bad feeling?" Forgive yourself for having the moment that you had, where you were unloving to yourself. You were simply unloving to yourself. You were simply, in that moment, unkind to yourself.

If you were angry at another person and you shouted at them, you were unkind to yourself and them. But your ability to move away from that angry person, meaning you, is far easier than you believe it to be.

Number one, you have to know where you are in any moment in time, emotionally. Are you steady in your emotions or are you upside down? Are you flying high and happy, or are you down in the dumps? Where are you emotionally a majority of the time?

A majority means 51%, it doesn't have to mean 90%. Although if you get to 90% and it's the right side up feeling, good. Reach for feeling good as a majority every day. Keep track of that kind of day, and the next day and the next will discover themselves in the same way. If you think you are having a zero feeling-day, then you are simply not paying attention, you are generalizing. We do not want you to generalize.

We want you, especially in those phases of your life where things are not going very well, to not generalize. We want you to say, "Well, at two o'clock I felt great." When someone asks, "What did you feel like at three o'clock?" Say, "I don't really remember, but at two o'clock I felt great" because that's the moment where you felt best. The whole rest of the day could have been thumbs down, but that is not what you need to talk about, it's not what you have to tell people.

So many of you tell stories for story's sake. It's unnecessary. It's also not good for you because you get whatever you talk about. You get whatever you talk about whether you talk about it to yourself in your mind, or whether you're talking out loud to somebody else, you get what you talk about.

Believe it or not, movies are people talking about things as well. If you are in earshot of a movie, make it a good one. Make it one that is pleasing to your ears, make it one that's pleasing to the inner mind because it is sensitive. Treat it with care and then watch what unfolds. That inner mind is the one that creates your life and it creates it based on what you think about, what you talk about, what you pay attention to, and how long you paid attention to it.

If you're all curled up on the couch and you're having a rotten day, it's OK. Just try not to extend it into an entire week- end or a week or a month or a year or phase of your life. Once you start going down that path, you will need help to move away from it.

In the moment that it occurs to you that you're having a bad day, that's the moment to say, "I don't have to feel this way." Don't blame it on another, "I would feel better if that person hadn't said what they said. Anybody would react in the same way." Not everybody would but it's all right that you did. Forgive yourself for it.

Tell yourself that you love yourself. Tell yourself that you're good. Tell yourself that you are loving. Tell yourself that you're happy, and then find things to support it. Remind yourself of those things and let that be what you think about.

You don't have to think about trash being left in the garbage can. You don't have to think about soiled linen stains that you can't get out. You noticed it, and it might have aggravated you, but it doesn't have to. It's an experience that you're having, and it does not have to be bound with negative emotion.

Negative emotion is the root cause of distress. They are not intertwined. Negative emotion can be stopped and if you stop it as soon as you recognize it then it does not find its way to distress, or deprivation, or a character trait.

You could be having a negative reaction, and it is a strange one for you, because you're rarely negative. You may say, "I don't know, I just flew off the handle, I never do that."

Someone else may have a similar day and people say, "It's just who they are, stay away from them, go the other way when they are mad." When people are mad, yes, go the other way. You don't want to experience their anger because you learn from it and you can be hurt by it.

If the angry person is you on that day, investigate a little bit, and ask yourself why. Then forgive yourself for displaying or reacting in a way that is not loving.

People are whoever they are in each moment in time, and you are who you are in each moment in time. If you collided or if you came together, you were you, they were they, and you had an experience.

That's all. Let yourself off the hook by saying it is not now, that whatever occurred is not happening now.

Forgive yourself for going backwards in your mind no matter how soon in the past it was. It's a nice thing to tell yourself, "I forgive myself for going backwards."

The mind has grown up in a world where you are taught to say, "I'm sorry, I didn't mean to, please forgive me." The mind knows what forgive means. "If you truly forgave me, you wouldn't still be angry" or similar statements are known by you. When you use the words "I forgive me" with yourself the mind reacts in a positive way.

This is far different than saying, "Oh whatever, I'm fine, I'll get over it." When you make that statement, the mind knows that you are really saying, "I'm holding on to this for a little while longer." That little while could extend to the rest of your life.

The mind follows a trail, and that trail is laden with thoughts and the thoughts are yours. If you step over that limb or that rock or that stream and you jump on another path, the mind simply goes with you. It follows that path for as long as you are on it. So, if you are on a bad one-way track in your mind, it's OK, but it's not the only one-way track.

Step over into the nicer one, and then once that feels comfortable, step over into the nicer one yet, and keep moving until you just have happy all around you. You might say it's difficult, we say it is not. It is a practice that allows happy to be easy. The first time you try it, it could be easy if you tell yourself that it will be.

We cannot teach human behavior any differently. This is how the human mind works. You think about one upsetting topic and then another thought like it comes. Then you stay there, and you stay there, and you stay there. You might briefly think of something else, but you will come back to that track. Or, that track widens and now you have several things that are bothering you all on your mind at once. That's the one-way track.

Those alternate ideas, those positive ideas that occur to you while steeped in aggravation was us, (although your Guide specifically) giving you a better thought - try this, think about this, look at this, focus on this. When you do, watch what happens.

If you are full of rage and you just happen to notice your favorite pair of shoes on the floor, look at the shoes and say, "Oh, those are my favorite shoes" and watch how the fury dissipates. You can snatch rage right back up again. We don't want you to, but so many of you do. However, you can flip flop your emotions if you choose to.

You could also see your favorite shoes on

the floor and then get angry that your shoes are left on the floor, whether you did it or not. You might scoop them up and storm up the steps and throw them in the closet.

You could however, in that moment say to yourself, "Those are my favorite shoes. Isn't it interesting, how in this moment where I'm so angry, I find something to look at that pleases me? These are my favorite shoes, or they're my shoes, or they are somebody's shoes, or there sits on the floor, a pair of shoes. Those shoes are black. Those shoes are fairly new. Those shoes are not mine. Those shoes are not my style, but they're shoes. Isn't it interesting how many different kinds of shoes there are? I wonder how many pairs of shoes are in this house alone? I know I own quite a few. I wonder if I counted them all up, how many would I have. Let me guess, I'm going to say 34."

Then wander about the house, the closets, the front stoop, the garage and find them all and count them because it gives you something to do that has nothing to do with anger. Just shift your gaze, shift your gaze, shift your gaze.

You can do it. We don't want you to work yourself up into rage and then try it for the first time, however. If you are in that dense emotion and you shift immediately out of it on the first try, then you probably were not full of rage, you were just angry, or possibly even annoyed.

We want you to try this when you are feeling confusion, frustration, just a tad bit of angry. We want all of you to practice on a little bit of sad like when you watch those commercials that make your eyes get all teary. In that moment, we want you to look across the room and just start talking to yourself about some object. Train yourself to swiftly move away from

sad, because too many of you let sad fall all the way down into depression. A little bit at a time, but all the way down.

We want you to train yourself out of sad, quickly. Start with using little things that don't matter. Songs are a good one. Sometimes song lyrics remind you of some terrible moment and they make you cry.

Shift your gaze, pick out an object and just start talking about it. "Well, there's a beautiful bag. Oh my luggage, I love my luggage. I think I owned probably four different sets of luggage in my life, and I'm not sure which one I love the best, but I like the small ones with the handle, with the rolling wheels. Oh I like the bags that are all full of colors. I love the bag that has my name on it. You know, I'm really not that particular, I have a variety and whenever I travel I just choose which-ever one stands out to me."

Just begin talking about something.

If you need to go outside so that you can talk aloud and really make it work then do it, and just tell whoever's in the room that you will be right back. If you have to say it angrily because you were in that angry mood, go ahead and do it. Then go outside and work yourself down from angry. Then come back in and act like you forgot you were angry in the first place.

If someone else is still angry, ignore it. How do you ignore it? Pick a different object and go walk around and go talk about that. You will find it easier and easier, and you might even laugh a little along the way at how easy it really is.

Why would you do this activity, though? We know that so many of you are going to argue with us in this moment and say, "But I need to get my point across. I didn't get what I wanted out of the conversation. It

was my last - whatever it was - and it broke. It was my grandmother's necklace, there is not another like it. That is something to be upset about. How can I not be upset about that? How can you tell me to not cry when my father just died? Or my puppy dog. I loved that puppy dog."

You can work yourself into sad real quick, can't you? You can work yourself out of it as well. We're not saying that objects and people don't matter, we would never say that. We think all life matters, all friendships matter. They matter so much that we want you to learn how to embrace them fully.

But truly, your grandmother's necklace if it breaks, could you have it fixed? Probably. Even if the glass on it shattered, you could have it fixed. It might cost you a little money, but you could. Or you could put it in a beautiful keepsake box and keep it. If it was something that you love to wear,

find a picture of yourself and make that a picture that you keep, showing how you wore it.

There's no better thing to lose than a bad

mood and a sad feeling.

There's nothing like the present to say this -
when you shift easily, you start to hear us
more clearly. When you do, we more easily
give you the idea that you might be looking
for, to salvage that thing that you thought
was broken or lost or forgotten.

Forgiveness is a word that the mind knows.
We want you to use it with yourself because
the mind will shift when you do. You might
not feel it right away, but if you make a
habit of it then you will find that there will
be less need eventually for you to use it.

"My lunch was terrible. I got so mad at the
waitress. I thought about it, though, and I

forgive myself. I forgive myself for being
angry at the waitress. I forgive myself for not
enjoying that lunch as much as I could
have. I forgive myself for leaving my shoes
all strewn about, because I know that
that's not how I care for my shoes. I forgive

myself for not making my bed today. I forgive myself for spending a little too much money at the grocery store. I forgive myself for not eating those vegetables before they got a little moldy. I forgive myself, I forgive myself, I forgive myself."

You don't have to be angry to use those words. You don't have to be in a in a temper tantrum to use those words. You don't have to be coming out of a temper tantrum or having symptoms that are present as you're trying to move away from that inner struggle. "Do I look up and smile or do I frown? Do I use a curse word or do I gently touch someone on the arm or the shoulder or the leg? Do I buy two ice

cream cones instead of one? Do I add a little note in the lunch bag, or not?" If you choose not, then say later, "I forgive myself for not doing that thing that would have felt good. I believe that I will next time."

We want you to make a habit of saying

those words to yourself. We want you to make a habit of saying without a specific example of frustration or annoyance, "I forgive me, I forgive me, I forgive me, I forgive me." You don't have to be in a bad mood to do it, you can simply choose a Saturday morning when you don't have too many things going on, to sit with your journal and write "I forgive me, I forgive me and I love..."

It's a beautiful journal prompt, I forgive me. Use different colored pencils and different scrolly letters, some capital, some lowercase, some bubble letters. Draw little lines and dots in the bubble letters, like

some do. Do smile faces or crowns or stars and decorate the page. I forgive me. I forgive me. I forgive me. I forgive me.

You could make a poem out of it or a song and sing it to yourself in the shower. "I forgive me. I forgive me, I forgive me. I forgive me. Scrub your hair. Scrub your hair. Forgive,

forgive. I forgive me. Scrub your hair, scrub your hair, wash the underarm. I forgive me. I forgive me." This is rather difficult to imagine through a book but add a little melody and re- read those words, you will get the idea.

Add a little show tune to it — a little quiet voice that builds and builds and open the arms up wide and add theatrical presence to your playfulness. You get the picture. Be brave. Be playful.

The words are so needed in the mind because you've learned as children, "Go say you're sorry" and you've had people

say, "I'm sorry" to you and you know how it makes you feel. Apologize to yourself, in other words but in an apology you are focusing on what you think you did wrong. "I'm sorry I shouted." What the inner mind hears is, "I have something to be sorry for and that something is that I shouted and I should feel bad."

The mind will then bring you things to feel bad about, more opportunities to shout because those were the words you used. Or it creates a belief that you ought to feel guilty about things. Then it starts substituting happy for feelings of guilt, or embarrassment. So we want you to say or sing playfully, "I forgive me, I forgive me, I forgive me. I forgive me." The general "I forgive me" removes the tendency to focus on the subject of what you are sorry for.

I forgave myself a hundred times today. This example too, is not the very best because

the words matter. The mind registers that you had one hundred things to forgive yourself about. Therefore, the present tense is always best. "I forgive me." By saying, "I forgive me" with a light and airy nature the mind will believe that it ought to be happy at being forgiven. It loses sight of any unhappiness from a specific subject in favor of choosing happy. "Well, I don't know what I did, but, now is the time to be happy."

Know in that moment you might feel silly for saying, "I forgive me." It's OK because when the mind is confused, as it may be on its way to changing, it will give you an emotion and it may chose silly. Ignore it and say, "I forgive me" anyway.

How often? Every day. For how long? Depends on where you are in life. If you're feeling pretty good, once or twice is sufficient. If you're going through a rough patch, 15 times a day is good. If you

can add positive emotion with it, then increase to 30. Your circumstances will change faster when you do. If you cannot muster, or haven't figured out how to muster, a positive attitude while saying the words, then keep it to 15.

Be playful about it and practice on small things like commercials, songs, small irritants.

Small irritants can be things that you notice that go on your to do list — I need to buy more shampoo, I need to clean out the garage, I need to mow the lawn. If you love to mow the lawn, then that one needs no cleaning up. But if you find mowing the lawn to be a chore, and you have that momentary disgruntled feeling of, "Ugh, time to mow the lawn" then use that as a moment to say, "I forgive me" or "I forgive me and I love to mow the lawn."

If you add something like that, excellent. "I forgive me, I love to mow the lawn" is far

different than, "I forgive me for being unhappy about mowing the lawn." The words and the tone, the vibration that you give to yourself - are opposites. Even if you don't love to mow the lawn, say "I forgive me" and the mind will settle down. It will stop bringing you irritating things to experience. Thoughts create things every single time.

Forgiveness is equal to stepping away from, only it lasts longer because the inner mind learns. It does take some time but don't let that be a deterrent because the time it takes could be twice before the inner mind alters itself and steps onto the other one-way track ahead of you and starts bringing you things that you are wanting to experience. You don't know when the mind is ready to shift. You will know when it has shifted because the mind simply stops being upset in that moment.

You will have more experiences of the opposite, things that cause you to smile, things that cause you to not even think about your emotion. Truly, when you are up, and awake, and having a beautiful day, you don't stop and say, "I'm having a beautiful day, maybe I should work a little harder at this." What you do say is, "Let's do more of it."

When you're having a bad day, the

emotional word shows up and you talk about it, "I was so pissed off, let me tell you why. Oh, I was so mad at her. Oh, my gosh, it hurts so bad, I just sat down and cried, I don't even know what to do. Oh, my God, I'm so confused, where do I go?" You add the emotional words.

On occasion, you say the F word or something like it because you've been taught to let off steam. We don't want you to let off steam, we want you to walk away from it and be happy that you did,

and then say, "I forgive me" coming out of whatever it was that you walked away from.

We love these little books, because it's just enough to give you examples and exercises or games to play to retrain the mind. We love teaching you in this way, it is our favorite thing to do. There is enjoyment around every corner. When your day is delightful, we can bring more things like it to you. Learn who your inner mind believes you to be and then emphasize it or intentionally alter it.

When your day is not so delightful, turn the page. Forgive yourself for needing to turn the page. Say it to yourself, let your inner mind hear you say, "I forgive me." It will know that it is forgiven, and it will jump over the stream and head down the path of happy.

Watch what happens when you playfully do these exercises. They retrain the mind to consistently favor a happy disposition. It is not temporary. The inner mind wants to hear us, wants our guidance. It wants to know what we know. We want you to hear us. The way to hear us consistently is to retrain the mind to become shallow in its emotional range.

Combining the techniques and exercises in this little book will open your mind to your ocular abilities. Remove worry, remove doubt, remove tendencies for anger or self-judgement. Learn to release anger in the moment and there will be less moments of an- ger. Your ability to hear us verbally will strengthen when you do.

engage with The Teachers

GOLD and PLATINUM Membership
Powerful opportunity to engage with The Teachers live with unlimited workshops and/or classes.

Private Readings with The Teachers:
With pin-pointed accuracy, they know what you need to know and how to bring clarity to your life. By appointment daily.

Signature Workshops
Designed as an introduction to The Essential Material and how to parter with your Guide to Self heal. They are the most powerful teachings on law of attraction and self-healing yet!

Channeled Classes
Live-virtual ongoing weekly classes with The Teachers on how to advance your intuitive abilities all the way to channeling and the concepts of self-healing and all the ways to do it.

praise for The Teachers

When I first heard Carol channel, I immediate- ly thought she sounded like a young Esther Hicks. Powerful teaching every time!

The teaching by The Teachers is extraordinary. I have learned – and unlearned! – so much. I cannot thank you enough.

The Grid just makes sense! Law of attraction seemed to be something in the ethers or just feel good way to think. I am so glad to have found Jeshua and their teaching. I get it!

Carol, I feel so blessed to have found you. The channeled reading I had with you changed my life. Never before have I felt to empow- ered!

Attunements are life saving for me! I have no more shy in me, I have a zest for life. I am now strong, healthy, active, and feel so alive!

My life has altered in every way imaginable since having attunements with The Teachers They healed my emotions, and they healed my body. I feel like a new person. Thank you, Carol for doing what you do.

about the author

Carol Collins is the channel for Jeshua the collective that many refer to simply as, The Teachers. Her abilities spontaneously manifested in March 2019. After nine months of quiet meditation "face spelling" was introduced as a means of direct communication followed by alpha-state verbal channeling. Through her, they teach about collective consciousness, manifesting with ease, health and wellness through natural healing, and advancing the natural ability to connect and communicate with your Guide – the Four Pillars of Learning that they call The Essential Material. She offers private sessions with The Teachers for readings and attunements daily, signature workshops, and classes frequently. She is a rising star among professional channelers.

To contact her please see her website: americas-medium.com or on all social media platforms as: America's Medium